I0517694

THE MORAL ARGUMENT

IS IT WORTH HAVING IN YOUR APOLOGETICS REPERTOIRE?

L. J. ANDERSON

LAMAD PRESS

Copyright © 2025 by L. J. Anderson

www.ljandersonbooks.com

Published by Lamad Press, PO Box 50785, Billings MT, 59105, www.lamadpress.com

ISBN 978-1-963291-06-3 (paperback) and 978-1-963291-07-0 (ebook)

All rights reserved.

No portion of this book may be reproduced in any form without written permission from the publisher or author, except as permitted by US copyright law.

Unless otherwise noted, Scripture quotations are from the ESV® Bible (The Holy Bible, English Standard Version®), © 2001 by Crossway, a publishing ministry of Good News Publishers. Used by permission. All rights reserved.

Book cover by L. J. Anderson

First edition 2025

CONTENTS

To Jenn,

For supporting me (and putting up with me)
in all my academic and authorly endeavors.

PREFACE

The book you are reading is the result of scholarly research presented in a format accessible to the general public. Normally, a work like this would not be published in this form. It would almost certainly appear as a journal article—technically accessible, but realistically out of reach for most Christians. This is simply because very few Christians who haven't attended Bible college read academic journal articles in their pursuit of God. However, many do read books.

Even pastors often find it difficult to engage with journal articles regularly, though they may have a large collection of books. Presenting research in book form—similar in depth and length to a journal article—means it can potentially reach a much broader audience. That is why virtually all of my journal-length writings are, or will be, published as short books. My goal is to provide solid academic research without requiring readers to locate or gain access to academic journals.

Additionally, I hope more authors and scholars will join me in this endeavor. Independent publishing offers many benefits and only a few significant drawbacks—namely, the lack of peer review and brand recognition. Until an author becomes well-known, they often depend on the credibility of the publisher's name. Peer review, for its part, plays an important role in academic publishing, acting as a gatekeeper to prevent poor scholarship from reaching publication.

However, peer review does not guarantee high-quality work, just as the absence of peer review does not necessarily imply poor quality. In many ways, true peer review begins after publication, when the broader academic community has the opportunity to evaluate and respond to the work. If that's the case, then an independently published book or article can undergo "organic" peer review through scholarly engagement and public critique, just like any traditionally published book provided it gains the necessary visibility.

While still largely untested, this publishing model shows promise as an alternative method of making academic research accessible. The majority of scholars continue to view independent publishing as significantly inferior to peer-reviewed articles or works released by traditional academic presses.

ABSTRACT

Have you ever wondered whether the existence of seemingly universal morals can serve as a faith-building and
evangelistic tool? In *The Moral Argument*, L. J. Anderson
challenges the widespread neglect of the moral argument
in contemporary apologetics, arguing that it deserves a re-
newed place in both academic and lay Christian discourse.
Historically, scholars have expressed skepticism about the
argument's effectiveness, often sidelining it in defenses of
the Christian faith. Yet, as moral questions become in-
creasingly central in cultural debates, might this argument
offer fresh apologetic power?

    The Moral Argument engages the historical develop-
ment of the argument, analyzes key objections and their
counterpoints, examines biblical support, and concludes
with a practical application section. While the argument
remains controversial, Anderson contends that its philo-

sophical and theological depth merits serious reconsideration.

INTRODUCTION

The general argument presented in this book was originally published as a chapter in my earlier work, *Contending for the Truth: A Biblical Look at Thirteen Contentious Doctrines*. However, I soon realized I had made a mistake in how that material was organized.

Typically, when essays are compiled into a single volume, they either share a common topic or have been published elsewhere individually. I did neither. I published them together as a single book, but the essays were unrelated in topic—connected only by their contentious nature. This presented a problem.

For instance, if someone were searching for content on the moral argument for the existence of God, they would likely never come across *Contending for the Truth*, despite it containing a dedicated chapter on the subject. The metadata simply couldn't support that many unrelated topics under one title. As a result, several solid arguments I had written on specific issues remained effectively hidden from the readers who might be looking for them.

To address this, I decided to make those chapters available individually, so that each could stand on its own and be more easily found.

This particular volume—*The Moral Argument*—explores a contentious apologetic argument, one that continues to divide scholars in terms of its effectiveness and relevance. While the argument is experiencing a resurgence of interest, it still occupies a relatively unreputable and marginalized position within academic circles.

Chapter One

A Brief History

IN MANY WAYS, EARLY Christianity, including Scripture itself, was focused on demonstrating that the God of the Bible is the one true God. This is because most of human history has been characterized by theism. It was exceedingly rare for someone in ancient times to have been an atheist. However, in the last few hundred years this has shifted. Atheism and agnosticism are now more prevalent than ever; thus the argumentation has needed to shift from proving that the God of the Bible is the one true God to proving that God exists to begin with. Many methods and arguments have been produced to attempt to prove this with one such attempt being called the moral argument.

The moral argument for God's existence tends to be more popular among non-scholarly Christians than those who are professional scholars/theologians. On the moral argument, theologian John Feinberg states, "This kind of argument isn't as popular among philosophers (even Christian ones) as the others, but it is very appealing to ordinary people. There is a certain commonsense plausibility to it, as one can attest from C. S. Lewis's version in *Mere Christianity*."[1] Feinberg goes on to say that, of all the rational arguments for God, the moral argument is "least likely" to be rationally compelling.[2] Does this mean that the moral argument is not worth pursuing when trying to convince nonbelievers about the existence of God? Is this even a fair representation of the moral argument? Interestingly, many contemporary theologians, who would now dispute Feinberg on this, view this lack of emphasis on the moral argument as a travesty. That said, it remains a rather unreputable argument for God's existence among academics. Despite its mediocre reputation in academic circles, this book will demonstrate that the moral argu-

---

1. John S. Feinberg, *No One Like Him: The Doctrine of God* (Wheaton, IL: Crossway, 2005), 199.

2. Ibid., 202. Feinberg argues here that the main value of the moral argument is bolstering a Christian's faith rather than being a convincing argument for taking an atheist from unbelief to belief in God.

ment is one of the most powerful tools for proving the reasonableness of God's existence, especially when paired with other arguments.

History of the Moral Argument

Before engaging with the moral argument itself, it is necessary to look at a brief history of it. This history can fairly effectively be split into two categories, pre-Kant and post-Kant. This is because many would argue that the eighteenth-century German philosopher Immanuel Kant invented, or at least initially systematized, the moral argument for the existence of God.

History Pre-Kant

Immanuel Kant may be the first person to deal with the moral argument systematically enough to be considered its originator. However, there were flavors of this argument as far back as Socrates, Plato, and Aristotle. Philosophy professors and authors David Baggett and Jerry Walls write, "We find in Plato the notion that things have goodness insofar as they stand in some relation to the

Good. The Good, Plato believed, subsists in itself."[3] This is essentially the view of Christianity only in Christianity the "Good" is the "good God, Yahweh." This idea can be found moving through significant historical Christian figures such as Augustine and Thomas Aquinas.[4] Other more modern philosophers took up various attempts at a moral argument which finally culminated in Immanuel Kant engaging with it in a major way.

Development Post-Kant

Since Kant first engaged heavily with the moral argument, there has been a back-and-forth between upholding the moral argument as worthwhile and thus developing it (as can be seen in C. S. Lewis's *Mere Christianity*) and holding the argument in such contempt that it was entirely ignored in many apologetics books (such as Alvin Plantinga's *God and Other Minds: A Study of the Rational Justification of Belief in God*). *Mere Christianity* is arguably the most famous attempt at a moral argument. However,

---

3. David Baggett and Jerry L. Walls, *The Moral Argument: A History* (New York: Oxford University Press, 2019), 9.

4. Ibid., 11.

it has also been met with criticism that is, in many ways, unfair.[5] William Lane Craig views the moral argument as the most effective argument for reaching his audiences at college and university campuses based on the response to it when it is presented.[6] In agreement with Craig's experience, non-scholarly Christians have fairly consistently accepted it as worthwhile, and there seems to be a resurgence of it among Christian scholars.

---

5. Christopher A. Shrock, "Mere Christianity and the Moral Argument for the Existence of God," *Sehnsucht: The C. S. Lewis Journal* 11, no. 1 (2023): 99-103.

6. Baggett and Walls, *The Moral Argument*, 2.

CHAPTER TWO

OBJECTIONS TO THE MORAL ARGUMENT

THERE ARE THREE MAIN objections to the moral argument, and they, generally, come from non-Christians. However, there are Christian philosophers who agree that these objections are valid, or at least provide enough reason not to pursue the moral argument as a good argument for the existence of God.

There Are No Universal Objective Morals

In contemporary times, this is likely the most common reasoning against the moral argument. Moral relativism—the view that each culture develops its own morals—holds sway in most Western countries. The fact that many morals seem to be shared by many different cultures is simply the result of human reason recognizing that certain things such as murder are not beneficial for society. There is no overarching power in the universe and one's truth is one's truth even if it runs counter to another person's truth. That said, there are different types of moral relativism. What is described above is a more traditional type similar to what you are likely to run into on the street. Some moral relativists, though, espouse the possibility that universal morals have come about through the process of natural selection as laid out in evolutionary theory.

Objective Morals Can Be Explained Naturalistically

The moral argument states that the only valid explanation for objective morals is some higher power that institutes a law that is above every other law. This can be a non-divine power in that a sufficiently advanced alien race could technically do this if they managed to unlock the ability to create life and instill it with these objective truths. Contrarily, since the nineteenth century, the common view of pretty much anything related to science and humanity comes from an evolutionary angle.[1] This counterargument to the moral argument suggests that ob-

---

1. Dale Eugene Kratt, "The Secular Moral Project and the Moral Argument for God: A Brief Synopsis History," *Religions* 14, no. 8 (2023): 985.

jective morals can come about via naturalistic methods. In other words, everything has come about by natural, selective processes. For example, anthropologists Oliver Curry, Daniel Mullins, and Harvey Whitehouse work toward proving a theory that suggests morals come about from the need to work together for mutual survival. They effectively demonstrated that sixty diverse communities across the world all hold seven moral beliefs universally.[2] This is interesting in that it is a relativistic theory that recognizes the problems with traditional moral relativism. As opposed to traditional moral relativism, this theory holds that there *are* universal morals and has demonstrated this quite effectively. We shall see in the next chapter that, though their data appears to be good, their interpretation of the data is flawed. Attempting to give a rational reason for seemingly universal morals, they actually provide excellent evidence for a theist to use.

I want to make note of two things before we move on. I am just going to lay them out briefly as to truly

---

2. Oliver Scott Curry, Daniel Austin Mullins, and Harvey Whitehouse, "Is It Good to Cooperate? Testing the Theory of Morality-as-Cooperation in 60 Societies," *Current Anthropology* 60:1 (2019): 54.

answer them lays outside of the scope of this book. First, mankind's ability to reason is itself problematic for any naturalistic theory. There is an entire set of apologetic arguments built around the idea that the ability to reason cannot have come about naturally by random chance.[3] Second, there is a historical and religious angle to look at. Historically, virtually every single people group has believed in a god or gods of some sort and from this belief, these people groups also upheld certain morals. Granted, sometimes the things done in the name of these deities has been horrific (i.e., child sacrifices), but it is still a significant bit of evidence from an apologetic standpoint. It is only recently that atheism has been more than severely marginalized. Even today, theism of some sort is the predominate view of the world. I will address this latter point a bit more in chapter four.

Begging the Question (On Both Sides)

Both sides of the debate regarding whether there are indeed universal, objective morals accuse the other of begging the question. Begging the question is a logical fallacy

---

3. William Lane Craig and J. P. Moreland, eds, *The Blackwell Companion to Natural Theology* (Malden, MA: Wiley-Blackwell, 2012), 351.

wherein someone argues for a specific conclusion based on a preconceived belief in the truth of the said conclusion. For example, I could say "Pineapple doesn't belong on pizza because pizza doesn't have pineapples." This is an extremely simplified example, but it demonstrates the point well enough. I need to provide *evidence* that demonstrates pineapple does not belong on pizza in order to logically make the claim that pineapple does not, indeed, belong on pizza. Similarly, from the secular viewpoint, the argument is that Christians only believe in universal morals because Christians already believe in God who created everything, made humans in his image, and is, himself, moral. Thus, Christians *assume* the existence of these universal morals based on the preconceived notion of the existence of a personal divine being. On the flip side, Christians accuse secularists of assuming that there are no universal morals because of their belief that everything came about by chance and natural processes. This challenge is often brought up as an impassible problem for the moral argument.[4] Contemporary Christian philosopher Dale Eugene Kratt exposes one particularly difficult barrier in the dialog be-

---

4. Feinberg, *No One Like Him*, 202.

tween Christians and secularists: "Many current secular thinkers refuse to engage with the theistic arguments or even acknowledge the history of the moral argument."[5] This is similar to the tendency to simply *ignore* the arguments and evidence from young earth creationists. It is hard to engage in debates with those who beg the question so much that they will not even engage with the opposing side.

CHAPTER THREE

COUNTER ARGUMENTS SUPPORTING THE MORAL ARGUMENT

T HE PREVIOUS SECTION DEMONSTRATED some of the major objections raised regarding the moral argument, but are these objections valid? The evidence suggests that the objections are not enough to reject the moral argument as a means of demonstrating the existence of God. Before hitting individual points, it is important to point out the discrepancy that can be seen in the lives of many who argue against universal, objective morals and instead hold to subjectivism in that they are often "later found promoting some moral cause."[1] Many of the most ardent moral relativists also hold certain moral positions as absolute despite the contradiction with their stated be-

---

1. Craig and Moreland, *The Blackwell Companion*, 394.

liefs on moralism. Another point of order before getting into specifics is what exactly is meant by "objective" moral values. William Lane Craig gives a good definition when he writes, "To say that there are objective moral values is to say that something is good or evil independently of whether any human being believes it to be so."[2] This is true; however, it is also important to note that objective moral values tend to be universally held except in very rare cases.

Significant Evidence for Universal Objective Morals

Universal, objective morals are not rare. In some sense, they are so obvious that most people do not even think twice about them. C. S. Lewis argues the case for objective morals by saying,

> But taking the race as a whole [as opposed to finding individual exceptions], they thought that the human idea of decent behavior was obvious to everyone. And I believe they were right. If they were not, then all the things we said about the war were nonsense. What

2. Craig, *Reasonable Faith*, 258.

was the sense of saying the enemy were in the
wrong unless Right is a real thing which the
Nazis at the bottom knew as well as we did
and ought to have practiced?[3]

The whole fight against the Nazis was predicated on the knowledge that what they were doing was morally wrong. Interestingly, when Nazi leaders began to be tried for their crimes, their defense lawyers argued for moral relativism (the idea that morality is determined by culture with no universals) and this defense was almost insurmountable in an era where moral relativism was taking a greater hold on the world. Philosophy professor and author J. P. Moreland states, "Individuals following the trial were shocked by how effective the Nazis' defense team was in arguing against the charges. How is that possible? What defense could be given for the indefensible?"[4] Ultimately, their defense was only defeated by appealing to a "law

---

3. C. S. Lewis, *Mere Christianity* (New York: HarperOne, 1952), 5.

4. J. P. Moreland, *Love Your God with All Your Mind: The Role of Reason in the Life of the Soul* (Colorado Springs: NavPress, 2012), 188.

above the law."[5]

Many different areas can be looked at to demonstrate these universally understood moral beliefs. One area is found in a study that attempted to prove the morality-as-cooperation theory. This study found, "In 961 out of 962 observations (99.9%), cooperative behavior had a positive moral valence."[6] The study did not test for any other areas of morality; however, the fact remains that certain things are universally held as morally good and things contrary to these are universally immoral.[7]

---

5. Ibid.

6. Curry, Mullins, and Whitehouse, "Is It Good to Cooperate?" 54. This article found that the seven areas that they specifically tested for (helping family members, helping group members, engaging in reciprocal cooperation, being brave, respecting one's superiors, sharing or dividing a disputed resource, and respecting others' property) were universally held as morally good and that the opposites of these things were universally seen as morally bad.

7. Not testing for other areas is a distinct problem with this article as it concludes that the morality-as-cooperation theory is sound even though there are other examples of universal morals that do not necessarily fit under the theory. Thus, the theory does not adequately deal with the various aspects of morality that need to be addressed when discussing the origins of morality.

Murder is another area that demonstrates a rather universal view, morally speaking. Justin Hogan-Doran, a senior counsel of the Australian Bar and an arbitrator in international and domestic arbitrations, states, "Whilst the crime of murder, and its equivalents, is clearly defined and subject to extensive jurisprudence in every jurisdiction, no attempt has been made to give this crime a definition at the international level."[8] The fact that a country makes something illegal does not necessarily mean that it is immoral; however, the fact that *every* jurisdiction understands murder as a problem that *needs* to be illegal suggests that murder is a universal, objective, moral evil. You could ask essentially anyone anywhere in the world whether it is wrong to murder someone and in almost all instances the answer to the question will be an emphatic "yes." Of course, the fact that murder happens means that humans are able to find ways of *justifying* the wrong, at least in their own heads. An interesting case study on this is

---

8. Justin Hogan-Doran, "Case Analysis: Murder as a Crime Under International Law and the Statute of the International Criminal Tribunal for the Former Yugoslavia: Of Law, Legal Language, and a Comparative Approach to Legal Meaning," *Leiden Journal of International Law* 11 (1998): 165.

the debate surrounding abortion. It is predicated on what constitutes a *human life*. The argument is never that we should have the right to murder. Instead, it is that the child in the womb is not, in fact, a person. As such, pro-abortion advocates sidestep their knowledge that murder is wrong by depersoning babies in the womb. Statements such as "It's only a clump of cells" are common. This allows a disconnect between murder and killing a fetus. Norman L. Geisler writes, "The pro-abortion position is dependent on the belief that the unborn is not an actual human pe rson."[9] Thus, the debate must necessarily revolve around what constitutes a human being. If it can be proven that babies in the womb are, in fact, human, then it is immediately evident that it is murder and thus wrong. This demonstrates that even those who advocate for a woman's right to kill the child in her womb understand that murdering humans is immoral, which makes a strong case for the universality of morals. Of course, this runs into the distinct problem of people being unwilling to acknowledge the truth. When everyone can have and does have their

---

9. Norman L. Geisler, *Christian Ethics: Contemporary Issues & Options* (Grand Rapids, MI: Baker Academic, 2010), 132.

own "truth," it is less reasonable to consider other points of view as being potentially valid. This is a direct product of the prevalence of moral relativism in Western society.

A final challenge with moral relativism is that, in practice, no one actually holds to it. Even the most ardent moral relativist believes in universal morals. The most obvious example is found in the idea of moral relativism itself. The concept is built on a universal idea that we all get to discover our own "truths." Yet, that is a universal claim that applies to *everyone*. Additionally, it is argued that my truths should not be imposed on anyone else's truths, and vice versa. This is self-refuting. It is very similar to the argument that many, including Christians, have today regarding judging others. Telling someone that they are being judgmental is itself a judgment. Overall, moral relativism logically undermines itself.

Naturalistic Explanations Fail on Numerous Counts

Naturalism cannot provide a good basis for any form of universal, objective morals simply because naturalism is necessarily a process of random chance and is subject to the idea of survival of the fittest. Apologist Paul Copan argues, "It is *theism* that furnishes the metaphysical resources to make sense of the instantiation of moral properties in the form of objective moral values, human dignity, human rights, and obligations."[10] A God who made humans in his own image, including knowing right from wrong, is the more logical approach to this problem. It allows for a solid foundation for objective morals which other non-theistic, or even non-personal theistic, theories cannot p rovide.[11]

Another problem is that those who hold to naturalism tend to uphold the inherent goodness of humans. This view purports that humans can and will achieve a utopia through the power of reason and scientific advancements. Similar to the previous argument, there is no *basis* for this belief. How are humans inherently good? At best, the natural world could produce humans that are inherently *neutral* moralistically speaking. In the animal kingdom, a king snake eating another snake is not *wrong*, it just *is*. However, the vast majority of humans are actively repulsed by the idea of eating another human. Why? Naturalism cannot

---

10. Copan and Moser, *The Rationality of Theism*, 153.

11. Andrew Ter Ern Loke, "A New Moral Argument for the Existence of God," *International Journal for Philosophy of Religion* 93, no. 1 (February 2023): 26.

sufficiently explain why this would be a problem. Killing and eating another human from a Christian perspective though is morally wrong because people are created in the image of God and thus have inherent value. From a naturalist angle, one could correctly argue that a serial killer who goes about killing "rival" males to take their wives as his own is not doing anything wrong. In reality, the killer would be demonstrating natural selection at its finest.

Dealing with the Begging-the-Question Problem

As mentioned previously, the begging-the-question problem of the moral argument is often seen as impassable. However, this is *exactly* how science is supposed to work. One is to come up with a hypothesis that can then be tested. The challenge is *not* that the initial hypothesis is made based on different factors. The problem lies in the willingness to accept evidence and the different interpretations of the results. The two above sections demonstrate, quite well, that the evidence is for the existence of God and against naturalistic explanations. The naturalistic view of morality should look precisely like what is seen in the animal kingdom. The strong rule and the weak perish. Yet, humans are not like this. Humans, as a general rule, *yearn* for justice to be done. People are driven to anger, fury, indignation, and sorrow when the weak and innocent are harmed. This is true in almost every situation. It is, fundamentally, not begging the question to have different hypotheses based on differing beliefs. In the initial discussion of this problem, I gave an example of begging the question in the form of pineapple belonging on pizza. If we were to take that same example and look at it from a different angle, I can *hypothesize* that pineapple does not belong on pizza simply because I do not like it. However, I then need to back that hypothesis up by looking at the evidence of what makes something a *pizza*. I would argue that, though I hate pineapple on pizza, there is no evidence that reasonably precludes pineapple from being on a pizza. My hypothesis, then, should change based on the evidence. This does not typically happen. For example, the morality-as-cooperation theory article discussed above hypothesizes that certain moral traits will be universally seen and that this would prove the viability of the theory. However, the writers fail to do a broad enough search on universal moral attributes. It only takes one universal attribute that is *not* connected to the idea of cooperation to demonstrate that the theory is insufficient. Yet, the authors do not look at other possible moral attributes. Going back to the idea that murder is considered morally wrong universally, we can see that murder does not fit in their seven tested areas.[12] Indeed, we can argue that murder being a universal moral belief goes *against* the theory because murdering outsiders is likely to be beneficial in many of the seven areas they tested. If someone is harassing my family members, I should be able to kill the person to help my family members out. However, this is *wrong* and arguably everyone knows it as is evidenced in the study. The writers are so focused on proving the theory that they cannot see the holes in the theory.[13] *That* is the problem, not the fact that we approach the problem with different hypotheses and theories.

---

12. To reiterate, these are helping family members, helping group members, engaging in reciprocal cooperation, being brave, respecting one's superiors, sharing or dividing a disputed resource, and respecting others' property.

13. This is why it is helpful to engage with people with different backgrounds and beliefs as it can help us see past the areas that are blocking our vision.

Chapter Four

Biblical Backing

O<small>NE OF THE MAJOR</small> strengths of the moral argument is its biblical backing. Often arguments for the existence of God have little to no reference to Scripture as they are philosophical in nature and are often only based on the use of reason. That said, the moral argument is, in a variety of ways, founded on what God himself has said. Of course, this can be seen as a negative thing as so often the argument is assumed to be invalid if Scripture is brought in. However, scriptural support should give Christians confidence to use the argument. Romans 1:18–23 says,

> For the wrath of God is revealed from heaven against all ungodliness and unrighteousness of men, who by their unrighteousness suppress the truth. For what can be known

about God is plain to them, because God has shown it to them. For his invisible attributes, namely, his eternal power and divine nature, have been clearly perceived, ever since the creation of the world, in the things that have been made. So they are without excuse. For although they knew God, they did not honor him as God or give thanks to him, but they became futile in their thinking, and their foolish hearts were darkened. Claiming to be wise, they became fools, and exchanged the glory of the immortal God for images resembling mortal man and birds and animals and creeping things.

This passage directly states that *everyone* knows there is a God; however, some suppress the truth by their unrighteousness. There will always be people who reject the sound understanding that God is the most reasonable explanation for the origin of the universe and life in general, but more specifically, there will always be people who reject that moral absolutes are actually absolute. Scripture tells Christians that everyone knows, deep down, that there is a God. Likewise, everyone knows deep down that there are universal, objective morals. This is also in Scripture. Romans 2:14–15 says,

> For when Gentiles, who do not have the law, by nature do what the law requires, they are a law unto themselves, even though they do not have the law. They show that the work of the law is written on their hearts, while their conscience also bears witness, and their conflicting thoughts accuse or even excuse them.

Gentiles, those who have not received the law, do the law *by nature* because it is *written on their hearts*. Thus, the reason murder is almost universally acknowledged as evil is that God's law, which states that murder is wrong, is written on everyone's heart. This is beneficial for us to know when giving the moral argument. The ones we are talking to *have* God's law written on their hearts. Whether they acknowledge said law is another question; however, we can reasonably expect that they know right from wrong, at least in a basic form. This is often described as the "natural law." This passage brings me back to a point I briefly mentioned in chapter two. Virtually all people groups throughout history have been theistic in some way and had a moral code. Romans 1 and 2 give the best explanation for this. Deep down, everyone knows there is a God. However, in most cases, instead of worshipping the one true God, mankind has pushed him out in favor of other gods, ones made of metal and wood and made in the likeness of things in the universe. Yet, even in mankind's rejection of God, there is evidence for a creator who has instilled his law on our hearts.

Additionally, Ephesians 4:19 reemphasizes Paul's argument regarding why certain people do the things that everyone knows are immoral. Ephesians 4:17–19 says,

> Now this I say and testify in the Lord, that you must no longer walk as the Gentiles do, in the futility of their minds. They are darkened in their understanding, alienated from the life of God because of the ignorance that is in them, due to their hardness of heart. They have become callous and have given themselves up to sensuality, greedy to

practice every kind of impurity.

Paul argues that the Gentiles walk as they do because they have become callous due to giving themselves over to their passions. This progression—from moral awareness to moral numbness—is something we can observe both historically and personally. Over time, repeated exposure to immoral behavior can dull the conscience, making what was once clearly wrong seem acceptable or even normal. I've experienced this personally. During my time in the Navy, I became heavily involved in viewing pornography. At first, I knew it was wrong, but over time, I found ways to justify it by telling myself things like, "everyone watches porn" or "it isn't hurting anyone." These rationalizations reflect the very callousness Paul warns about: a conscience dulled by repeated indulgence. What was once morally troubling became normalized. This example shows how rejecting God's moral law, even subconsciously, leads to confusion and a loss of sensitivity to right and wrong. It's a vivid reminder that the moral law written on our hearts can be suppressed, but not erased.

Chapter Five

Application

How does the moral argument help Christians live out their lives as Christians? Is it truly valuable for someone to spend their time learning this enough to be able to use it or teach it? Additionally, if one does learn it, should it be used on its own or with other arguments for the existence of God?

The most obvious application of the moral argument is for evangelism. Learning the moral argument is valuable in demonstrating the reasonableness of the existence of God. As with other arguments or methods of evangelism, it is *not* a guaranteed way to evangelize. You and I cannot lay out the moral argument so well that our listeners cannot help but to believe in God. However, it is a valuable way to attempt to reach non-believers for Christ or at least to begin the process of moving some from being an atheist or agnostic to being a theist.

The second area that the moral argument is valuable for is its ability to increase one's faith. It is a reasonable argument for the existence of God. Since the general bent of the world right now is to assume that God does not exist and ridicule those who *do* believe, it provides an additional way for one to be confident in their belief in God.

The Moral Argument is Stronger Together

It is true, in a sense, that we can never convince a non-believer through argumentation that God exists. There is no one-size-fits-all argument that proves beyond a shadow of a doubt that God does, indeed, exist.[1] This is *especially* true if God is not already at work in the non-believer. However, in many, maybe even most, cases, God *is* at work. There is typically a reason someone is arguing against the existence of God. The challenge, then, is presenting an argument that is both meaningful and logical when given the opportunity. However, some arguments will work better than others. One person may find the moral argument to be utterly convincing while another thinks there is nothing of value there and would instead

---

1. Moreland, *Love Your God with All Your Mind*, 159.

respond to the ontological or some other argument. Thus, the best way to argue for the existence of God is either a cumulative effect (having the space necessary to give several arguments)[2] or having a "repertoire" of individual arguments to pull from depending on the situation. In both scenarios, having multiple avenues of "attack," as it were, is only beneficial to the argument for God's existence. David Baggett and Jerry Walls put it this way, "We believe the moral argument possesses a unique appeal that may well make it the most powerful of all theistic arguments—at least for many."[3] It is worth having this argument in one's repertoire simply because for many it will be the most powerful argument for God.

---

2. This is the method most often used in apologetics books.

3. Baggett and Walls, *The Moral Argument*, 2.

A BRIEF CALL TO ACTION

If you found value in this book, please consider leaving an honest review on your favorite book review site (Amazon, BookBub, Goodreads, etc.). Reviews are tremendously helpful to authors. They are, in many ways, the lifeblood of a book and I highly appreciate each one that I receive.

Also, if you are interested in receiving updates on books, book reviews, and other short teachings that I publish, you can follow me on:

- Facebook (Meta): L. J. Anderson at www.facebook.com/profile.php?id=61553506423559

- YouTube: L. J. Anderson at www.youtube.com/@ljandersonbooks

- My website: www.ljandersonbooks.com

ALSO BY L. J. ANDERSON

Books

- *Contending for the Truth: A Biblical Look at Thirteen Contentious Doctrines*

Short Books

- *Theology and Apologetics: An Examination of How and Where They Intersect*

- *The Inerrancy of Scripture: An Overview and Defense* (coming soon!)

- *Scientific Naturalism and Old Earth Creationism: Are They More Reasonable Alternatives to a Young Earth?* (coming soon!)

BIBLIOGRAPHY

Anderson, L. J. *Contending for the Truth: A Biblical Look at Thirteen Contentious Doctrines*. Billings, MT: Lamad Press, 2025.

Baggett, David, and Jerry L. Walls. *The Moral Argument: A History.* New York: Oxford University Press, 2019.

Craig, William Lane. *Reasonable Faith: Christian Truth and Apologetics.* Wheaton, IL: Crossway, 2008.

Craig, William Lane, and J. P. Moreland, eds. *The Blackwell Companion to Natural Theology*. Malden, MA: Wiley-Blackwell, 2012.

Curry, Oliver Scott, Daniel Austin Mullins, and Harvey Whitehouse. "Is It Good to Cooperate? Testing the

Theory of Morality-as-Cooperation in 60 Societies."
Current Anthropology 60:1 (2019): 47-69.

Feinberg, John S. *No One Like Him: The Doctrine of God.*
Wheaton, IL: Crossway, 2005.

Geisler, Norman L. *Christian Ethics: Contemporary Issues & Options.* Grand Rapids, MI: Baker Academic,
2010.

Hogan-Doran, Justin. "Case Analysis: Murder as a Crime
Under International Law and the Statute of the International Criminal Tribunal for the Former Yugoslavia: Of Law, Legal Language, and a Comparative Approach to Legal Meaning." *Leiden Journal of
International Law* 11 (1998): 165-181.

Kratt, Dale Eugene. "The Secular Moral Project and the
Moral Argument for God: A Brief Synopsis History." *Religions* 14, no. 8 (2023): 982-1004.

Lewis, C. S. *Mere Christianity.* New York: HarperOne,
1952.

Loke, Andrew Ter Ern. "A New Moral Argument for the Existence of God." *International Journal for Philosophy of Religion* 93, no. 1 (February 2023): 25-38.

Moreland, J. P. *Love Your God with All Your Mind: The Role of Reason in the Life of the Soul.* Colorado Springs: NavPress, 2012.

Moser, Paul K., and Paul Copan, eds. *The Rationality of Theism*. New York: Routledge, 2003.

Shrock, Christopher A. "Mere Christianity and the Moral Argument for the Existence of God." *Sehnsucht: The C. S. Lewis Journal* 11, no. 1 (2023): 99-120.

www.ingramcontent.com/pod-product-compliance
Lightning Source LLC
Chambersburg PA
CBHW061327120626
46546CB00007B/2703